This book is to be returned on or before the date above.
It may be borrowed for a further period if not in demand.

TOPIC
LOAN

Essex County Council
School Library Service

CONQUERORS & EXPLORERS

This edition:
© **Book Life 2015**
Book Life
King's Lynn
Norfolk PE30 4LS

First edition
2006 © Aladdin Books Ltd.
PO Box 53987
London SW15 2SF

ISBN 978-1-910512-07-4

Cover Design by:
Matt Rumbelow

Cover Photo by:
Zhu Difeng/shutterstock.com

Title Page Photo by:
Richart777/shutterstock.com

Illustrators:
Francesca D'Ottavi,
Alessandro Bartolezzi,
Lorenzo Cecchi,
Susanna Addario,
Claudia Saraceni –
McRae Books, Florence, Italy

BookLife

CONQUERORS

& EXPLORERS

HEROIC **H** HISTORY

JIM PIPE

BookLife

CONTENTS

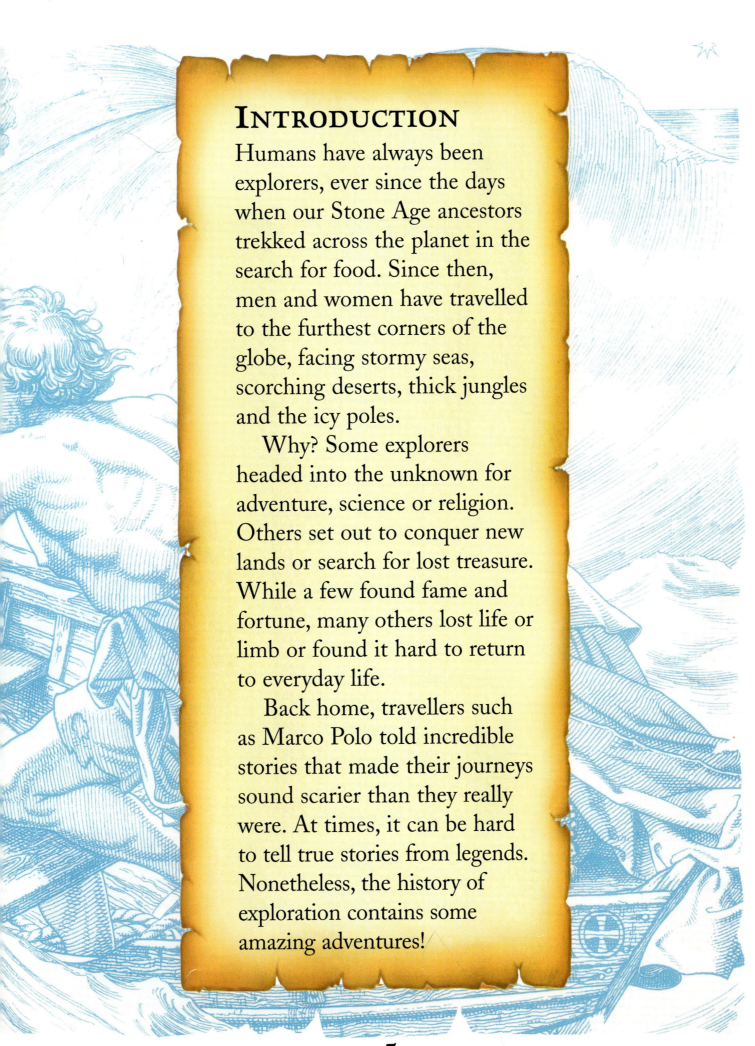

INTRODUCTION

Humans have always been explorers, ever since the days when our Stone Age ancestors trekked across the planet in the search for food. Since then, men and women have travelled to the furthest corners of the globe, facing stormy seas, scorching deserts, thick jungles and the icy poles.

Why? Some explorers headed into the unknown for adventure, science or religion. Others set out to conquer new lands or search for lost treasure. While a few found fame and fortune, many others lost life or limb or found it hard to return to everyday life.

Back home, travellers such as Marco Polo told incredible stories that made their journeys sound scarier than they really were. At times, it can be hard to tell true stories from legends. Nonetheless, the history of exploration contains some amazing adventures!

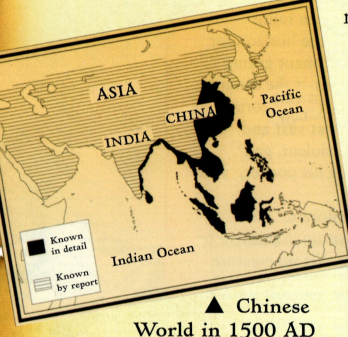

▲ Adventurers risked life and limb braving stormy seas, deserts and mountains.

PART 1: INTO THE UNKNOWN – WHY EXPLORE?

Humans have always been explorers. Some travellers just wanted an adventure. Kings and generals went in search of foreign lands to conquer. Missionaries travelled far and wide to spread their religion. Merchants sought out new trade routes, while scientists looked for unknown plants and animals.

▲ Chinese World in 1500 AD

▲ Islamic World in 1500 AD

Separate Worlds ▶
Until the 15th century, when sea captains from Europe found new routes to America and Asia, many parts of the world were cut off from each other.

Early Explorers
Over 30,000 years ago, Stone Age hunters trekked across the planet following great herds of mammoths.

By 8000 BC, humans were living in almost every part of the world.

Do aliens exist?

Ptolemy's Map

Lousy Maps! ▶
For hundreds of years, most explorers were at the mercy of wind and water. Few had maps to guide them and most of these were very inaccurate.

Ptolemy's map, used until the 15th century, shows a continent joining Africa and China that never existed.

Explore, Then Conquer
Many 16th-century European explorers were followed by conquering armies. They claimed the new lands for their king, ignoring the fact that people had already lived there for thousands of years.

▲ **European Exploration in 1490 AD**

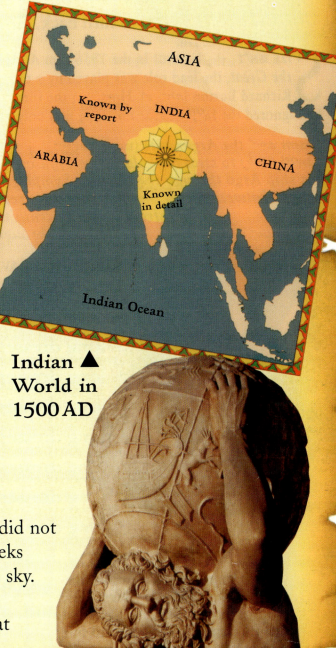

Indian ▲ World in 1500 AD

◀ Strange Beasts
In the past, people explained things they did not understand with stories. The ancient Greeks imagined that the giant Atlas held up the sky.

Early sailors described huge monsters living in distant seas. Today, we worry that outer space may be home to scary aliens!

Atlas

ANCIENT EXPLORERS

Almost 5,000 years ago, Egyptian explorers sailed down the Nile in papyrus ships. By 500 BC, traders from Carthage had sailed down the west coast of Africa. The Romans traded with India and China, but America was unknown to the rest of the world until Vikings landed 1,000 years later.

▲ Alexander the Great
In just 20 years, the Greek king Alexander the Great conquered all the land between Greece and India. When he died in 323 BC, he still had plans to reach the "Great Ocean" that ran around the edge of the world.

◀ Egyptian Travels
The first known explorer was the ancient Egyptian Harkhuf. In about 2250 BC, he travelled south along the Nile to the land of Punt, bringing home ivory and jewels.

Papyrus ship

Midnight Sun
In 325 BC, the ancient Greek explorer Pytheas sailed north to Iceland in search of copper and tin. In the Arctic summer the Sun shines day and night and Pytheas called it the "Midnight Sun".

▼ Jason and the Argonauts

In Greek legend, Jason steers his ship Argo through clashing rocks on his way to steal the golden fleece. Legends such as this may be based on sailors' voyages around the Mediterranean.

▲ **Silk Road.** From 100 BC, merchants travelled across Asia on the Silk Road, a route joining China and the Mediterranean.

The Silk Road

Watch Out! ▶

Homer's poem *The Odyssey* may have warned Greek sailors of dangers at sea. The hero of the poem, Odysseus, battles with witches, one-eyed giants, hurricanes and whirlpools during his 10-year voyage home. Some historians think the story describes the Mediterranean Sea, others the Atlantic Ocean.

Odysseus

TRAVELS IN THE EAST

From the 7th century AD, a new religion, Islam, spread quickly across the Middle East, Africa and Asia. Muslim pilgrims (followers of Islam) travelled far and wide, and Muslim sailors were famed for their seafaring skills. In 1405, Chinese admiral Zheng He led a fleet of 63 junks and 28,000 men to India and East Africa, carrying scientists as well as soldiers. He returned home with a rich cargo of ivory, pearls, spices – and a giraffe!

Night sky

▼ Early Navigation
The Chinese invented the compass in the 3rd century AD, but it was not used in Europe until 900 years later. To find north, European sailors relied on the stars.

▼ Sailors' Tales
The legends of Sinbad were probably based on the experiences of Muslim sailors in the Indian Ocean.

▼ **Chinese junk**

▲ **Marco Polo**
In 1271, 17-year-old Marco Polo travelled with his father and uncle to the court of Kublai Khan, the Chinese Emperor. Polo then travelled some 39,000 km around Asia before returning to Venice in 1295. He wrote a book about the amazing things he had seen, such as coal, paper money and asbestos.

Muslim ▶ mapmakers put their holy city, Mecca, in the middle of their maps.

Chinese Explorers
The Chinese did little exploring as they thought China was the centre of the world. However, Buddhist monk Fa Xian crossed the Gobi desert in the 5th century AD.

▲ Sea Raiders
The Vikings were great sailors. They sailed south as well as west, attacking towns in the Mediterranean and the Black Sea.

Longships ▶
Long and narrow, the Viking longship or "dragon boat" could survive the stormy seas of the Atlantic. Ships carried whole families along with their pigs, cattle and sheep.

PART 2: AMERICA – THE VIKINGS
In 980 AD, the Viking Eric the Red was banished from Norway. Sailing west across the Atlantic, he arrived in Greenland.

Twenty years later, his son, Leif Ericsson, sailed even further west. After a stormy voyage, Leif landed on a wooded island, which we now know as Newfoundland. Leif's crew spent the winter here, the first Europeans to reach America.

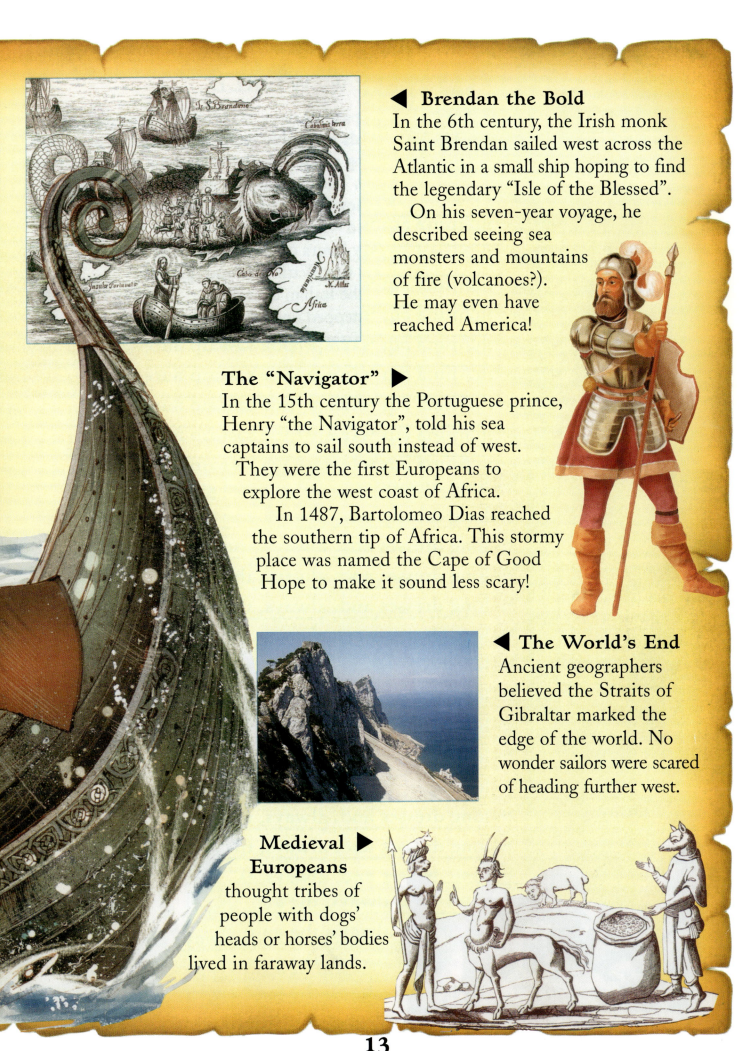

◀ Brendan the Bold

In the 6th century, the Irish monk Saint Brendan sailed west across the Atlantic in a small ship hoping to find the legendary "Isle of the Blessed".

On his seven-year voyage, he described seeing sea monsters and mountains of fire (volcanoes?). He may even have reached America!

The "Navigator" ▶

In the 15th century the Portuguese prince, Henry "the Navigator", told his sea captains to sail south instead of west. They were the first Europeans to explore the west coast of Africa.

In 1487, Bartolomeo Dias reached the southern tip of Africa. This stormy place was named the Cape of Good Hope to make it sound less scary!

◀ The World's End

Ancient geographers believed the Straits of Gibraltar marked the edge of the world. No wonder sailors were scared of heading further west.

Medieval ▶ Europeans

thought tribes of people with dogs' heads or horses' bodies lived in faraway lands.

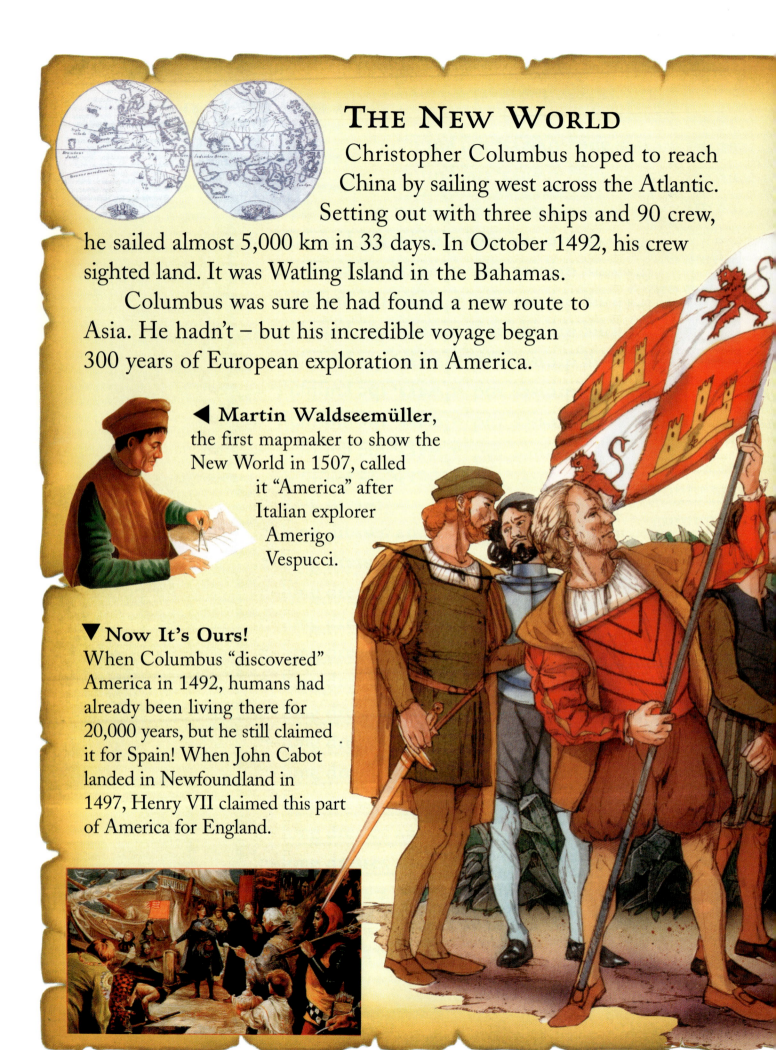

THE NEW WORLD

Christopher Columbus hoped to reach China by sailing west across the Atlantic. Setting out with three ships and 90 crew, he sailed almost 5,000 km in 33 days. In October 1492, his crew sighted land. It was Watling Island in the Bahamas.

Columbus was sure he had found a new route to Asia. He hadn't – but his incredible voyage began 300 years of European exploration in America.

◀ **Martin Waldseemüller**, the first mapmaker to show the New World in 1507, called it "America" after Italian explorer Amerigo Vespucci.

▼ **Now It's Ours!**
When Columbus "discovered" America in 1492, humans had already been living there for 20,000 years, but he still claimed it for Spain! When John Cabot landed in Newfoundland in 1497, Henry VII claimed this part of America for England.

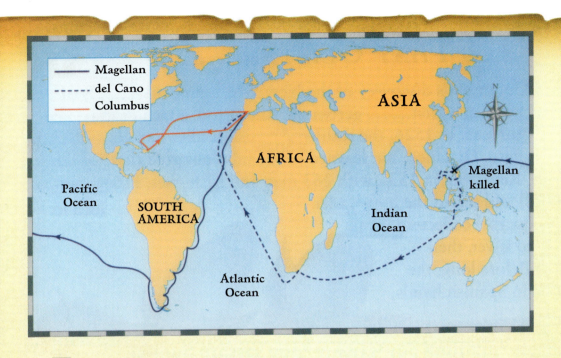

◀ **All Change!**
Magellan's voyage finally proved that the world was round and not flat. Columbus' journey brought America into contact with the rest of the world.

▼ **Columbus** thought he had reached the Indies (Asia), so he called the local Arawak people "Indians".

Around the Globe

In 1519, Ferdinand Magellan left Spain with five ships and 241 men. After sailing around South America and across the Pacific, Magellan was killed in a fight. But one of his ships, led by Sebastián del Cano, reached Spain in 1522, the first to sail around the world.

▲ **A Cruel Conqueror**
Columbus forced hundreds of the gentle Arawaks into slavery. His crew also brought deadly diseases that wiped out 250,000 islanders in 15 years.

THE CONQUISTADORS

Columbus was soon followed by the "Conquistadors", Spanish adventurers who flocked to the New World seeking fame and fortune. In 1526, Francisco Pizarro crossed the mountains into Peru (*map p.18*). With just 168 men, he destroyed the peaceful Inca civilisation in less than a year.

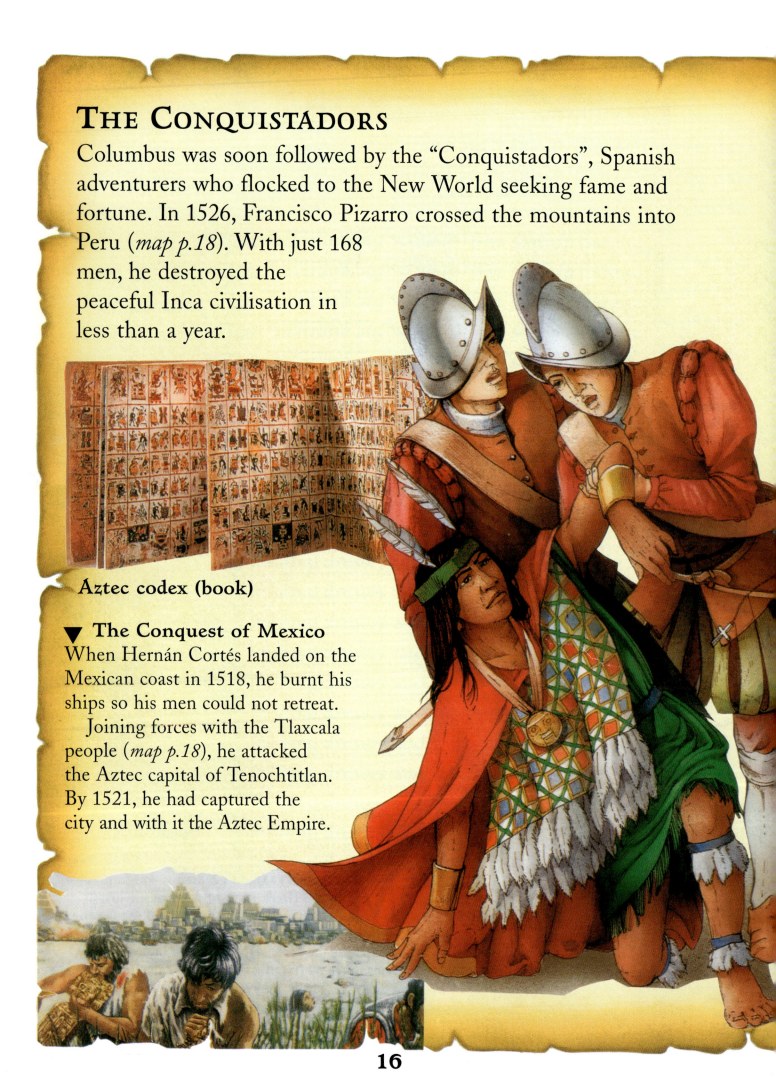

Aztec codex (book)

▼ **The Conquest of Mexico**
When Hernán Cortés landed on the Mexican coast in 1518, he burnt his ships so his men could not retreat.

Joining forces with the Tlaxcala people (*map p.18*), he attacked the Aztec capital of Tenochtitlan. By 1521, he had captured the city and with it the Aztec Empire.

Stone vs Metal

The Aztec warriors' stone weapons were no match for Spanish swords and cannons. Then millions died after catching European diseases such as smallpox.

Pizarro orders the death of Atahualpa.

◀ A Dirty Trick

Pizarro kidnapped the Inca leader, Atahualpa, who promised to fill a room with treasure if Pizarro let him go. But after he had seized 15 tonnes of gold and silver, Pizarro murdered his captive.

▲ Greedy for Gold

The Conquistadors searched in vain for "El Dorado", the legendary kingdom filled with gold. Determined and ruthless, they carried out many brutal attacks on the local people. Some tribes were so angry at the Spanish greed, they poured molten gold down their captives' throats.

Inca family

ACROSS AMERICA

In 1542, Francisco Orellana was part of an expedition trapped in the Amazon jungle. Orellana's party drifted downstream in search of food. Too weak to row back, they kept going. They reached the Atlantic eight months later, having travelled 8,000 kilometres down the Amazon River.

Journey to the Pacific ▶
In 1804, Meriwether Lewis and William Clark were the first Europeans to explore the North American interior. They rafted their way up the Missouri River, trekked across the Rockies, then floated downstream to the Pacific before heading back to St Louis.

Amazon ▶
Orellana named the Amazon River after fighting a tribe of female warriors, who reminded him of the Greek legend of the Amazons.

River Routes
Rivers provided the easiest way of crossing America. In 1682, French explorer René-Robert La Salle travelled down the Mississippi River from Canada to the Gulf of Mexico.

▲ **Indiana Jones** is perhaps the most famous movie explorer. Never seen without his fedora hat and flight jacket, the brave professor seeks out lost treasures in jungles and deserts.

NORTH AMERICA

Fort Chipewyan

Peace River

St Louis

Mississippi

New Orleans

Mackenzie
Lewis & Clark
La Salle

◀ **Native Guides**
In 1793, Scots fur trader Alexander Mackenzie was the first European to cross North America. After a failed attempt to find the Northwest Passage, he canoed 1,000 kilometres up the Peace River. With the help of Native guides, he trekked overland to the Pacific.

▲ **Settlers** – Lewis and Clark opened the way for thousands of European settlers. Backed by the US army, they took land from the Native Americans already living on the Great Plains.

MONSTER OR MYTH?

For hundreds of years, sailors brought home tales of hideous monsters. Most were just animals that no one had seen before, such as crocodiles and giant squid. Today, we wonder what strange creatures lurk in the ocean deep, the last unexplored wilderness on Earth.

▲ Scylla and Charybdis
In the legend of Odysseus, the hero must sail between Charybdis, a whirlpool that will suck his ship down to the ocean deep, and Scylla, a monster with six heads.

◀A Serpent?
Marco Polo describes seeing a giant serpent with "claws like a lion and eyes bigger than loaves". Today it is called a crocodile!

▼ Movies often feature monsters!

In a Whirl
Whirlpools can drown sailors by sucking them underwater, but few are strong enough to sink a big ship.

◀All in the Mind? ▶
Early explorers were terrified by tales of giant squids and other monsters. Today, people are afraid of meeting a giant shark or the Loch Ness Monster.

Seaman's Superstitions ▶

Sailors had good reason to be afraid. As well as being sunk in a storm, there was also danger from dying of thirst or being wrecked on a rocky coastline.

Many sailors were superstitious. Some believed that if they killed an albatross it brought bad luck for the rest of their life.

◀ Mermaids?

The legend of mermaids, beautiful women with the tail of a fish, are probably based on sightings of real creatures such as manatees or seals. The cries of these animals can sound very human and they sit on rocks, just like mermaids.

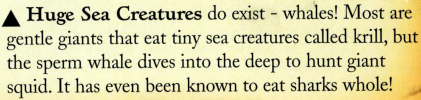

▲ **Huge Sea Creatures** do exist - whales! Most are gentle giants that eat tiny sea creatures called krill, but the sperm whale dives into the deep to hunt giant squid. It has even been known to eat sharks whole!

PART 3: ASIA – THE SEARCH FOR SPICES

In 1497, Portuguese sailor Vasco da Gama achieved what Columbus had failed to do – find a sea route to Asia. Da Gama sailed east around the southern tip of Africa and across the Indian Ocean.

Da Gama failed to impress the wealthy ruler of Calicut with the goods he offered, but still headed home with a rich cargo of spices. On his voyage home, however, da Gama lost two ships and 55 men.

▲ **Hot Stuff**
European traders could earn a fortune selling Asian spices, such as pepper, cinnamon, cloves and nutmeg, which were used in cooking and in medicines.

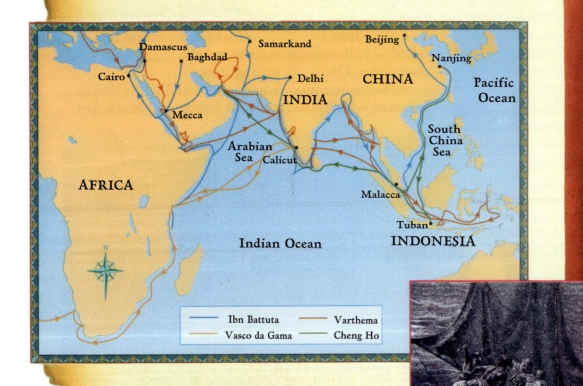

Ibn Battuta — Varthema
Vasco da Gama — Cheng Ho

Damascus, Baghdad, Samarkand, Beijing, Nanjing, Cairo, Mecca, Delhi, CHINA, Pacific Ocean, INDIA, Arabian Sea, Calicut, South China Sea, AFRICA, Malacca, Tuban, Indian Ocean, INDONESIA

Battuta the Wanderer ▶
From 1325-47, Muslim pilgrim Ibn Battuta saw more of the world than anyone before, travelling 120,000 km around Africa, Arabia, India and China.

Muslim Pilgrims ▶
Thousands of Muslims travelled far and wide to reach the holy city of Mecca.

In da Gama's Footsteps
By travelling in disguise as a Muslim, in 1506 Ludovico Varthema became the first European to reach the "Spice Islands" (now part of Indonesia), the original home of the spices nutmeg and cloves.

◀ **Trade and Conquest**
By the 17th century, many European countries had set up trading posts in Asia.
Armies followed the merchants and within 200 years there were European colonies in India, China, the Philippines and Indonesia.

Arab dhows

Arab Technology ▶
In the late Middle Ages, Arab merchants introduced triangular sails to European sailors. These new sails allowed ships to sail out of the Mediterranean and across the great oceans.

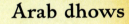

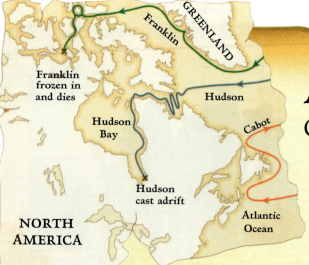

A FROZEN ROUTE TO ASIA

Other explorers searched for a route to Asia around the north of Canada. In 1610, English explorer Henry Hudson reached what is now Hudson Bay. Stuck in the ice during winter, many of his crew became sick. In the spring, they mutinied. Hudson, his son and seven others were set adrift in a small boat. They were never seen again.

◀ Not One, But Two
In 1728, Danish explorer Vitus Bering proved that Asia and America were separate continents by sailing through the Bering Strait (named after him).

Nansen's Icy Trip ▶
The sea route around the north of Canada is known as the Northwest Passage. Norwegian explorer Fridtjof Nansen was the first to sail through it in 1903-06. The first merchant ship crossed the passage in 1969, 350 years after Hudson!

◀ Polar Terrors
Polar explorers faced many dangers. In Antarctica, temperatures can plunge to -84° C in winter. Howling winds reach speeds of up to 320 km/h and icebergs can sink even large ships. In the Arctic, a hungry polar bear will attack anyone who gets too close!

Polar bear

Stuck in the Ice
In 1845, Sir John Franklin led a British expedition to find the Northwest Passage. When his ships got frozen in the ice, Franklin and 128 crew members died of hunger, cold and disease.

Frostbite ▶
One of the worst perils for Arctic explorers was frostbite. As the body freezes it becomes black and swollen and in time, fingers, toes, ears and noses may drop off.

◀ Search Party
Over the next 20 years, 39 expeditions were sent to to try and find Franklin. In 1859, Leopold McClintock's search party found a note written by Franklin's officers and a sad trail of skeletons. In the 1980s, scientists found bodies of the crew preserved in the icy soil.

Leaping Laptev ▼
When Russian explorer Khariton Laptev's ship got stuck in the ice in 1742, Laptev and his crew made it to shore by leaping across the icebergs for two days!

Survival Skills
Though Inuits knew how to survive in the Arctic, early explorers did not learn their survival skills.

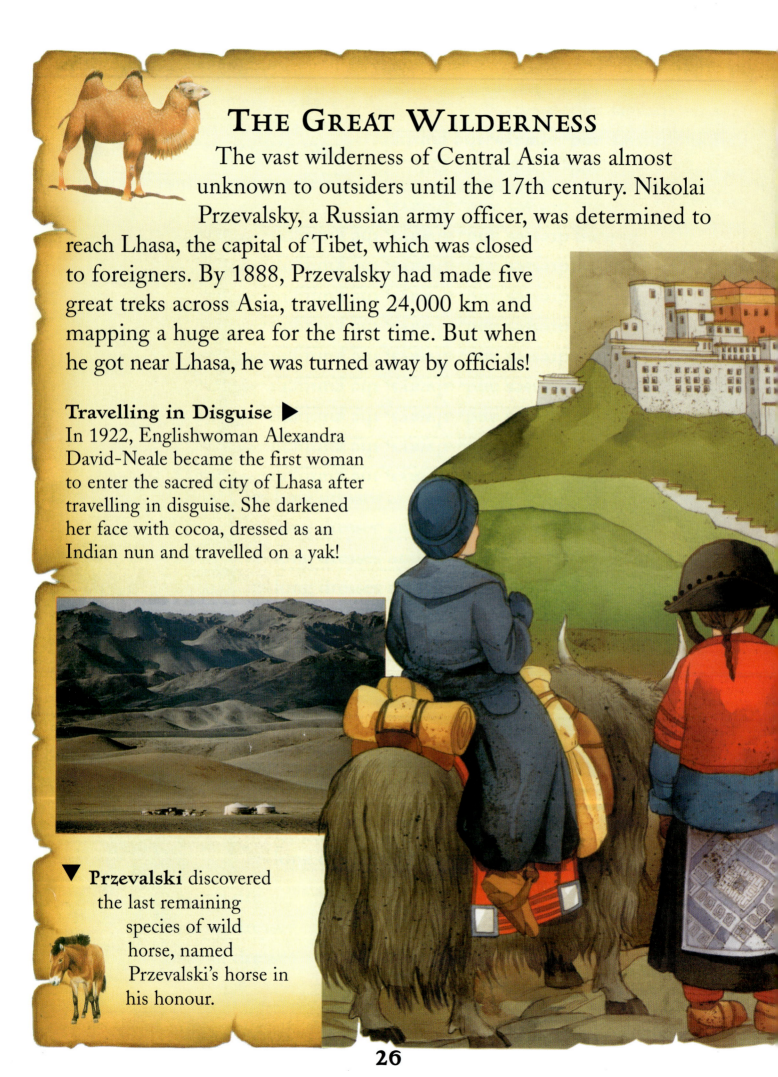

THE GREAT WILDERNESS

The vast wilderness of Central Asia was almost unknown to outsiders until the 17th century. Nikolai Przevalsky, a Russian army officer, was determined to reach Lhasa, the capital of Tibet, which was closed to foreigners. By 1888, Przevalsky had made five great treks across Asia, travelling 24,000 km and mapping a huge area for the first time. But when he got near Lhasa, he was turned away by officials!

Travelling in Disguise ▶

In 1922, Englishwoman Alexandra David-Neale became the first woman to enter the sacred city of Lhasa after travelling in disguise. She darkened her face with cocoa, dressed as an Indian nun and travelled on a yak!

▼ Przevalski discovered the last remaining species of wild horse, named Przevalski's horse in his honour.

Fantastic Journey ▶

One of the most famous storybook journeys is made by Lemuel Gulliver, hero of Jonathan Swift's *Gulliver's Travels* (1726). Gulliver visits the island of Lilliput, inhabited by tiny people.

A Land Far Away

◀ **A Land Far Away**
Przevalski mapped Mongolia 150 years ago, but people still use "Outer Mongolia" and "Timbuktu" (on the edge of the Sahara desert) to describe places that are a long way away.

On Foot

In 1866, Nain Singh travelled almost 2,000 km through Tibet in disguise, mapping the route to Lhasa. He measured his journey by counting his paces using the beads on a rosary.

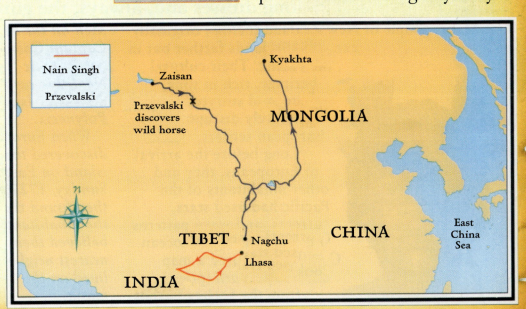

Nain Singh
Przevalski

Kyakhta
Zaisan
Przevalski discovers wild horse
MONGOLIA
TIBET
Nagchu
Lhasa
CHINA
East China Sea
INDIA

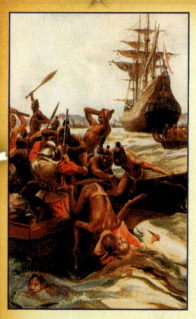

PART 4: THE PACIFIC – HEADING SOUTH

In three great voyages, James Cook explored more of the Earth's surface than anyone else in history. In his first voyage in 1770, he discovered Australia. Cook then explored the Pacific, and sailed around Antarctica (without ever spotting it!). Sadly, Cook's third voyage to find the Northwest passage ended in disaster: he was killed by Hawaiians after a row over a stolen boat.

Pacific Firsts

• In 1642, Dutchman Abel Tasman discovered New Zealand and Tasmania.

• In 1801, Matthew Flinders charted the entire coast of Australia.

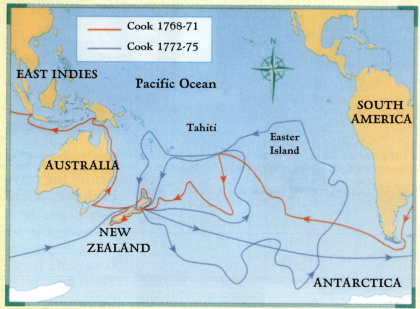

Cook 1768-71
Cook 1772-75

EAST INDIES
Pacific Ocean
SOUTH AMERICA
Tahiti
Easter Island
AUSTRALIA
NEW ZEALAND
ANTARCTICA

Maori

◀ Island Hoppers

From 400 AD, Polynesian islanders spread out across the Pacific, hopping from one island to the next.

By 1200 AD, they reached New Zealand, becoming the Maori people we know today.

Giants! ▶

Captain Cook marvelled at the giant statues on Easter Island. People here are over 3,000 km from their nearest neighbours!

◀Daniel Defoe's novel *Robinson Crusoe* (1719) spread the myth that Pacific islanders were savage cannibals.

Kon-Tiki

Raft Adventure▶
In 1947, Norwegian sailor Thor Heyerdahl sailed his raft *Kon-Tiki* across the Pacific to prove that ancient peoples from South America might have settled Polynesia.

◀ Fruity Cure
Cook fed his crew pickled cabbage and lemon juice to stop them getting scurvy, a disease which made sailors' teeth fall out before killing them.

▲ Spreading Disease
Sadly, Pacific islanders who were friendly with European sailors often caught devastating diseases such as smallpox and measles.

INTO THE OUTBACK

The wild interior of Australia, known as the Outback, is a tough place to survive in. In 1860, Robert Burke and William Wills' expedition tried to cross Australia from south to north. They battled through deserts, forests and swamps and reached the north coast.

On the way back, however, they ran out of food. Mad with fever, they walked in circles through the desert until they died from starvation.

◀ Vanished!

German explorer Ludwig Leichardt hoped to cross Australia from east to west. He hardly took any food as he planned to live off the land like the Aborigines. Sadly, he was a hopeless bushman. He was forced to turn back after trekking just 800 km in seven months. Leichardt set off again in 1848, but simply vanished into the Outback.

▼ Surviving the Outback

As well as the scorching heat and a lack of water in the deserts of Central Australia, explorers had to beware of poisonous snakes, spiders and scorpions. In northern Australia, crocodile-infested swamps and mountains slowed down many expeditions.

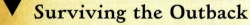

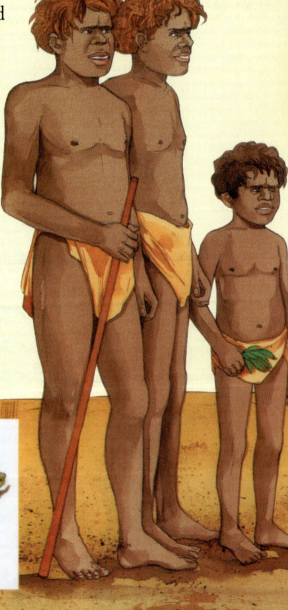

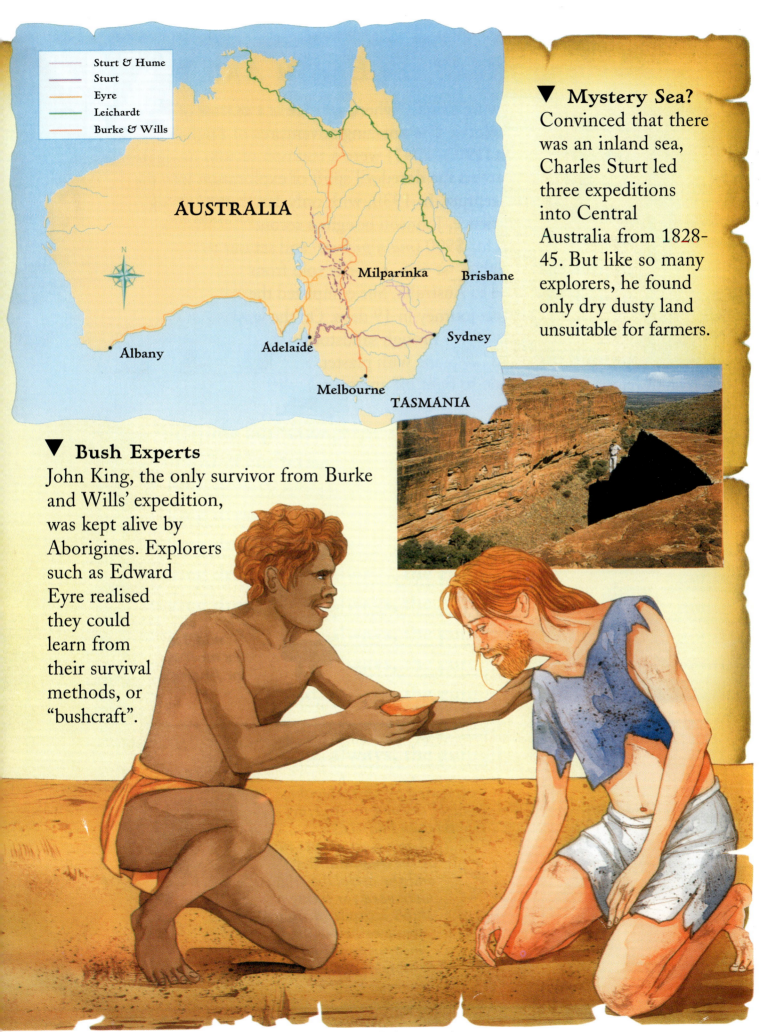

Sturt & Hume
Sturt
Eyre
Leichardt
Burke & Wills

AUSTRALIA

Milparinka
Brisbane

Albany
Adelaide
Sydney

Melbourne
TASMANIA

▼ Mystery Sea?

Convinced that there was an inland sea, Charles Sturt led three expeditions into Central Australia from 1828-45. But like so many explorers, he found only dry dusty land unsuitable for farmers.

▼ Bush Experts

John King, the only survivor from Burke and Wills' expedition, was kept alive by Aborigines. Explorers such as Edward Eyre realised they could learn from their survival methods, or "bushcraft".

WHERE AM I GOING?

Getting lost is every explorer's worst nightmare, whether in a jungle, out at sea or in the air. In 1930, English aviator Amy Johnson flew her Gypsy Moth solo all the way from England to Australia in just 19 days. Despite flying over unfamiliar jungles, mountains, deserts and shark-infested seas, she didn't lose her way. It was an amazing feat of navigation.

Sir Francis Drake's compass

▼ Davy Jones' Locker

To sailors, Davy Jones is the evil spirit of the deep who appears before storms and shipwrecks. "Davy Jones' Locker" is the bottom of the sea, the final resting place of drowned sailors and sunken ships.

Sextant

◄ Sextant

After 1731, the sextant was used to find a ship's latitude (its north-south position).

Finding Your Way

Ancient sailors found their way by observing the stars, tides and winds. Arab seafarers were first to use quadrants and astrolabes to work out latitude. These measured the angle of the Sun above the horizon.

Quadrant

Astrolabe

Lost! ▶

Many explorers have failed to return home: Vitus Bering got shipwrecked (1741), Robert Scott (*right*) froze in icy conditions (1911) and Amelia Earhart (1937) vanished while flying over the Pacific.

Amelia Johnson's Gypsy Moth

▼ Pure Paradise

The 1933 novel *The Lost Horizon*, set in the mystical Kunlun Mountains, gave the world a new word, "Shangri-La", which means a paradise on Earth.

Lines of **longitude** and **latitude** are used to plot a ship's position.

Time and Distance ▶

Longitude is the east-west position on the surface of the Earth. As the Earth spins once every 24 hours, distance can be measured in time difference, but only with a very accurate clock called a chronometer, which first appeared in the 18th century.

PART 5: AFRICA – UP RIVER

Mungo Park had never been to Africa when he was asked to explore the Niger River. On his first attempt he bravely marched into the Sahara and spent four months in an Arab gaol before he even got to the river. In 1805, he set off with 40 others. Just eight were still alive when he reached the Niger. Park drowned when his boat was attacked by tribesmen.

1793 Map of Africa

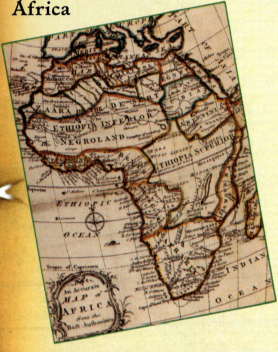

▲ **It's a Mystery!**
Scotsman Mungo Park followed the Niger for 1,300 km and proved that it flowed east. But he had also hoped to reach Timbuktu, a city said to be paved with gold.

Belief in such legends and poor maps show how little Europeans knew about Africa in the 1800s.

◄ **Across the Sahara**
In 1838, Réné Caillié trekked across the Sahara by camel and finally reached Timbuktu. Instead of golden palaces, he found only mud huts!

Missionaries ▶

Explorers in Africa and South America were soon followed by Christian missionaries. While some missions were peaceful, others helped European powers to steal land from the local peoples.

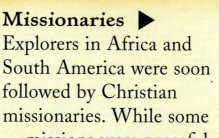

In 1858, ▶

Burton and Speke's party found the source of the Nile, which flows 6,700 km through the desert.

◀ **Mungo Park is attacked**

The Slave Trade ▼

Some explorers went to Africa to make money from slaves. From the 1500s to the 1800s, 12 million Africans were shipped across the Atlantic to sugar and cotton plantations in the New World. Conditions on board ship were so horrific that 1.5 million Africans died on the voyage.

Slave Ship

Money Troubles

Richard Burton and John Hanning Speke set off with 200 porters and an armed escort of 30 men. But when the money ran out, the porters ran off!

LOST IN THE JUNGLE

In 1855, David Livingstone had crossed Africa from coast to coast and discovered the Victoria Falls on the way. But by 1871, no one had heard any news from him for three years. Reporter Henry Stanley went to look for Livingstone. Tracking him down at Ujiji on Lake Tanganyika, Stanley put out his hand and said, "Dr Livingstone, I presume".

Mystery King ▶
In the 15th century, Portugal sent several expeditions to rescue Prester John, a Christian king said to rule a kingdom in Ethiopia. He never existed, but the legend brought Europeans to Africa.

◀ **What To Wear?**
Réné Caillié and Swiss explorer Jean-Louis Burckhardt travelled around North Africa by dressing up as Arabs. Stanley wore special clothing – boots, safari jackets and a pith helmet. Deep in the jungle, Mary Kingsley wore a tight-waisted dress and an umbrella to shield her from the Sun.

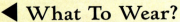

Livingstone was attacked by a lion in 1844, almost went deaf due to a fever and had his boat tipped over by a hippo. No wonder people thought he might be dead!

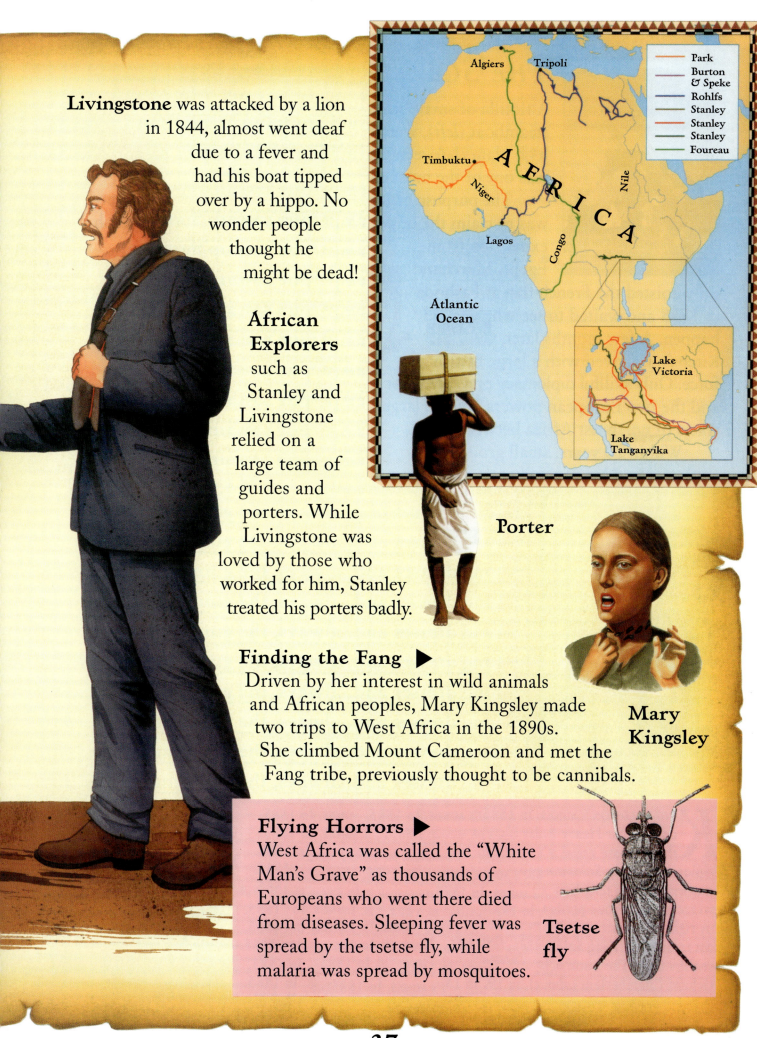

Park
Burton & Speke
Rohlfs
Stanley
Stanley
Stanley
Foureau

Algiers   Tripoli

AFRICA

Timbuktu

Niger

Nile

Lagos

Congo

Atlantic Ocean

Lake Victoria

Lake Tanganyika

African Explorers such as Stanley and Livingstone relied on a large team of guides and porters. While Livingstone was loved by those who worked for him, Stanley treated his porters badly.

Porter

Finding the Fang ▶
Driven by her interest in wild animals and African peoples, Mary Kingsley made two trips to West Africa in the 1890s. She climbed Mount Cameroon and met the Fang tribe, previously thought to be cannibals.

Mary Kingsley

Flying Horrors ▶
West Africa was called the "White Man's Grave" as thousands of Europeans who went there died from diseases. Sleeping fever was spread by the tsetse fly, while malaria was spread by mosquitoes.

Tsetse fly

THE SCRAMBLE FOR AFRICA

From the 1870s onwards, European powers greedily divided up Africa among themselves, known as the "Scramble for Africa". Explorers such as Henry Stanley and Pierre de Brazza were hired to trick local chiefs into handing over their land.

In a race with Britain to grab land near Fashoda in 1897, Frenchman Jean-Baptiste Marchand led an expedition carrying a steamboat hundreds of kilometres across western Africa.

A Land of Riches? ▲
Books such as *King's Solomon's Mines* (written in 1885 by H. Rider Haggard) depicted Africa as a "lost world" full of riches. The reality was less romantic – Europeans saw Africa as a source of cheap labour and a place to sell their goods.

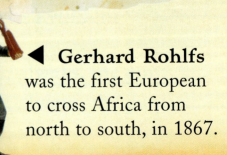

◄ **Gerhard Rohlfs** was the first European to cross Africa from north to south, in 1867.

Portable Boat

Stanley explored Lake Victoria on the 12-m long boat the *Lady Alice*. This could also be split into sections and carried overland.

Explorer for Hire

Already famous for finding Livingstone, in 1874 Henry Stanley followed the River Congo down to the sea and later discovered the "Mountains of the Moon" described by Ptolemy 2,000 years earlier. Less heroically, in the 1880s Stanley helped King Leopold of Belgium grab a large part of Central Africa.

▼ A Race to Conquer

In just 35 years, the European powers divided up almost all of Africa. Only Ethiopia and Liberia remained independent. The map below shows Africa in 1913. The red and blue lines mark the British and French race to Fashoda.

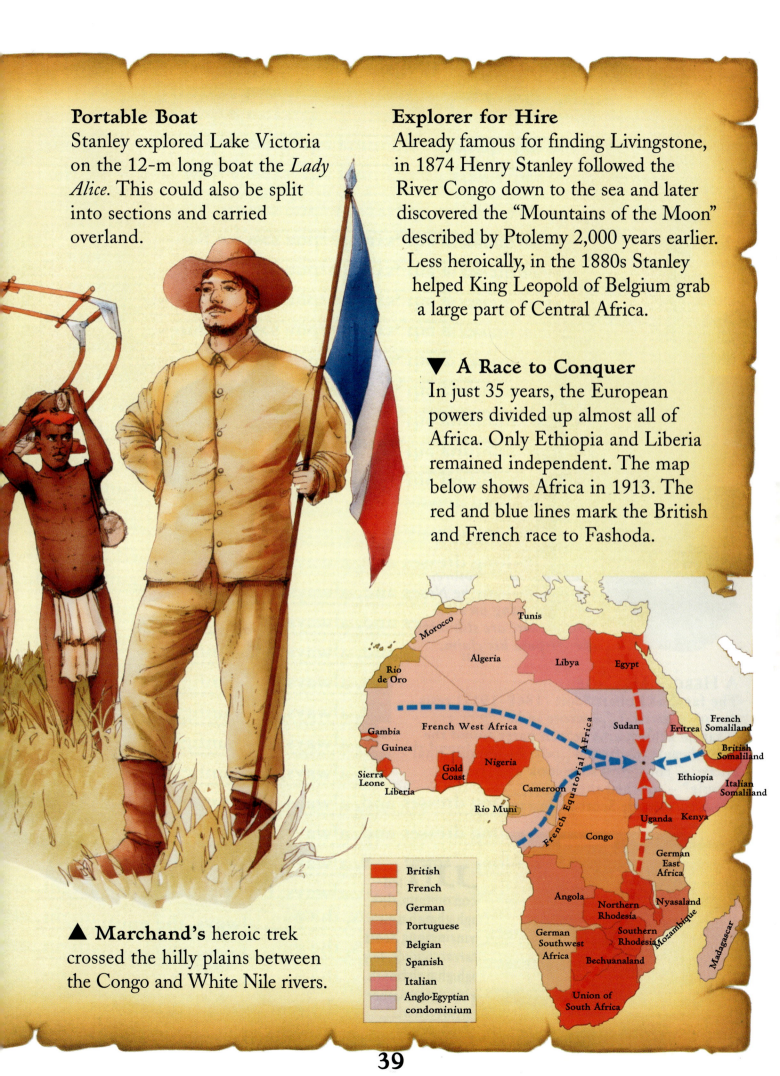

▲ **Marchand's** heroic trek crossed the hilly plains between the Congo and White Nile rivers.

Morocco · Tunis · Algeria · Libya · Egypt · Rio de Oro · Gambia · French West Africa · Sudan · Eritrea · French Somaliland · Guinea · Nigeria · British Somaliland · Sierra Leone · Gold Coast · Ethiopia · Italian Somaliland · Liberia · Cameroon · Rio Muni · French Equatorial Africa · Uganda · Kenya · Congo · German East Africa · Angola · Northern Rhodesia · Nyasaland · German Southwest Africa · Southern Rhodesia · Mozambique · Bechuanaland · Madagascar · Union of South Africa

British
French
German
Portuguese
Belgian
Spanish
Italian
Anglo-Egyptian condominium

PART 6: THE FINAL FRONTIER – RACE TO THE POLES

In October 1911, two rival expeditions set off in a race to the South Pole. Norwegian Roald Amundsen's party used skis and dog sleds. Moving quickly across the ice, they reached the South Pole on 14 December.

English explorer Robert Scott arrived a month later. Already worn out from dragging heavy sleds, two of his men died in terrible blizzards. Scott and two others froze to death in their tent.

Robert Peary

"Mine at Last"!
Americans Robert Peary and Matthew Henson were the first explorers to reach the North Pole in 1909. It was Peary's eighth attempt to get there!

▼ **A Heroic Message**
Amundsen won the race to the Pole, but Scott's brave attempt made him a hero. A search party found his diary next to his frozen body, which later became a best-selling book (and later a film).

◀ An Epic Voyage

Ernest Shackleton hoped to cross the Antarctic on foot. When his ship *Endurance* was slowly crushed by ice in 1915, he led his men to Elephant Island.

Shackleton then set off in a tiny boat, sailing 1,400 km across the stormy Atlantic before crossing mountainous South Georgia island to reach help.

Antarctic routes

Wisdom of the Inuits ▶

Amundsen learned from the Inuit peoples of the Arctic how to use dogs and sleds on the ice. The dogs' thick fur helped them survive in the freezing conditions while the ponies used by Scott soon died from the cold.

Arctic Legends ▼

Until Peary's journey in 1909, people argued about what was at the North Pole. In 1577, English explorers thought they had found a dead unicorn in the Arctic circle – it was a Narwhal, a mammal with a long twisted tooth.

In the early 1900s, people still believed that the Arctic might be a tropical paradise or a home to terrifying monsters!

HIGHER AND DEEPER

Asked why he wanted to climb Mount Everest in 1924, one climber said, "Because it's there". It wasn't until 29 May 1953 that Tenzing Norgay and Edmund Hillary became the first to make it to the top, the highest place on Earth!

Crampons

Ice pick

▼ **Edward Whymper** became interested in climbing after making sketches of the Alps. In 1865, he was first to climb the treacherous Matterhorn, but four of his team were killed on the way down.

A Tough Challenge
Between 1920 and 1952, seven major expeditions had tried and failed to reach the top of Everest.

Hot Stuff

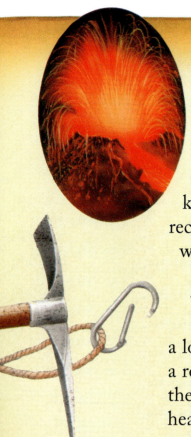

Several scientists have been killed or hurt while studying volcanoes, but a robot known as *Robovolc* has recently been built that will be able to explore inside the rim of a volcano.

However, it will be a long time before even a robot can journey into the bubbling 1200° C heat of a live volcano.

▲ Verne's journeys

In his novels *Journey to the Centre of the Earth* (1864) and *Twenty Thousand Leagues Under the Sea* (1870), Jules Verne imagined life deep below ground and at the bottom of the ocean.

Today, just five per cent of the ocean deep has been explored – so who knows what lurks down there!

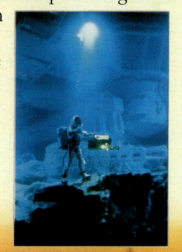

Dive, Dive!

In 1776, American David Bushell built the *Turtle*, one of the first submarines. It could stay underwater for 30 minutes and moved using a propeller turned by hand.

Turtle

Trieste

Viewing dome

On the Bottom

In 1960 Jacques Piccard and Don Walsh first reached the deepest point in the ocean, the Marianas Trench, in the *Trieste*. The 10,916m descent took them almost five hours, but sadly they forgot to take a camera! Modern submersibles such as *Deep Flight One* have wings that allow these craft to "fly" underwater!

Deep Flight One

OUT INTO SPACE

The space age began in 1957, when Sputnik I, the first man-made satellite, was launched into orbit. In 1961, Yuri Gagarin became the first human being to travel in space, and by 1969 Neil Armstrong and Buzz Aldrin had set foot on the Moon.

Since then unmanned space probes have landed on Mars and Venus and flown beyond the Solar System, and astronauts have lived on space stations. Where will we go next?

Men on the Moon? ▶
Galileo Galilei first looked at the Moon through a telescope in 1609, but for centuries after, people imagined finding exotic creatures on the Moon. In 1969, US astronauts finally proved there were no moon-men, only rocks!

Saturn V rocket

The International Space Station

Big Bucks ▲
The cost of putting rockets like Saturn V into space led to the space shuttle, but each shuttle flight cost $500 million!

Robot Explorers

The cheapest way to explore space is to use robots. In June 2008, the Phoenix Mars Lander began digging below the surface of Mars to look for water, vital to life.

Little Green Men ▶

For hundreds of years, writers have dreamed up horrible-looking aliens, like this creature from the star Sirius drawn in the 18th century. But there is no reason why they will look anything like us!

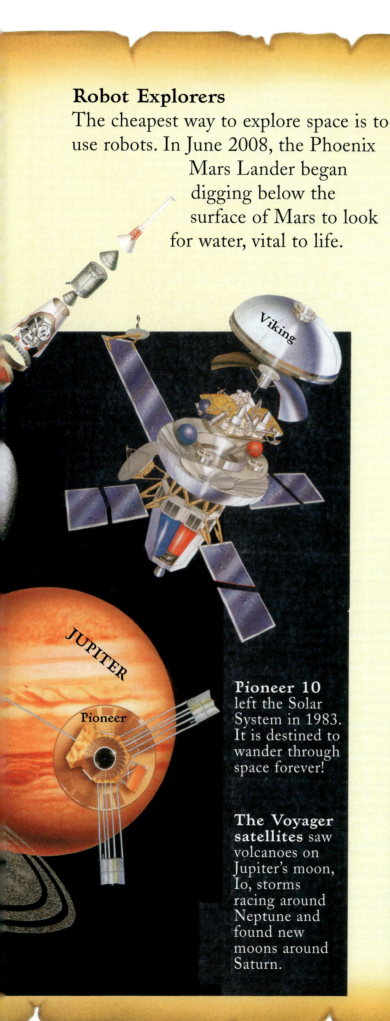

Viking

JUPITER

Pioneer

E.T.

Star Wars?

If we meet alien lifeforms, will they be friendly, like E.T., or will they wipe us out?

Pioneer 10 left the Solar System in 1983. It is destined to wander through space forever!

The Voyager satellites saw volcanoes on Jupiter's moon, Io, storms racing around Neptune and found new moons around Saturn.

▼ Space, the Final Frontier

For over 40 years, Star Trek has remained the most popular fantasy about space exploration. Like great explorers of the past, the crew of the Starship Enterprise "boldly go where no one has gone before".

EXPLORERS GLOSSARY

Aborigines – The original peoples of Australia.

Astrolabe – An instrument used by Arab sailors for working out latitude (*right*).

Bathyscape – A deep-sea vessel.

Cannibal – A person who eats the flesh of other people.

Caravan – A group of merchants travelling with animals such as camels.

Chronometer – A very accurate clock used for working out longitude at sea (*right*).

Compass – An instrument used to find north.

Conquistador – A Spanish conqueror in Central and South America in the 1500s.

Dhow – An Arab ship with a triangular sail (*far right*).

Glacier – A mass of ice that slowly moves downhill like a frozen river.

Iceberg – A huge lump of ice that has fallen off the end of a glacier.

Ice Floe – A small iceberg (*left*).

Junk – A Chinese sailing ship.

Latitude – Where you are on the Earth's surface, north or south of the equator.

Longitude – Your east-west position on the Earth's surface.

Magnetic Pole – The place on the Earth's surface to which all compass needles point.

Mermaids – The half-women, half-fish of legend may have been based on sightings of sea cows (*right*)!

Missionary – Someone who travels to spread their religion.

Navigation – Finding your way.

New World – The European term for America after its discovery.

Satellite – Spacecraft put into orbit around the Earth.

Sextant – A navigational instrument used for measuring the angle of the stars or Sun.

Submersible – A vessel that can operate underwater.

Whirlpool – A strong swirling current usually produced by ocean tides or very strong winds.

EXPLORERS TIMELINE

40,000 BC Early people spread out across the world.

c.2300 BC Harkhuf explores the upper Nile.

329 BC Alexander the Great reaches India.

308 BC Pytheas sails north to the Arctic Circle.

c. 150 AD Ptolemy draws his famous atlas, *Geography*.

3rd century AD The Chinese develop the magnetic compass.

6th century AD St. Brendan voyages across the Atlantic.

750 Polynesians (above) settle New Zealand.

c. 1000 Vikings settle in Greenland and America.

1275 Marco Polo arrives in China.

1325–1349 Travels of Ibn Battuta across Africa and Asia.

1404–1433 Zheng He's voyages around the Indian Ocean.

1434–1460 Henry the Navigator's captains explore the west African coast.

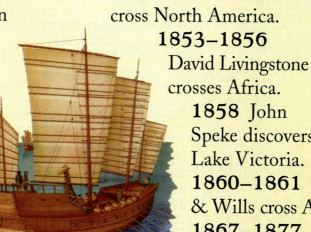

1492–1493 Columbus reaches America.

1498 Vasco da Gama arrives in India.

1522 Magellan's (*left*) expedition is the first to sail around the globe.

1518-1522 Cortés conquers the Aztecs.

1531–1535 Pizarro conquers the Incas.

1542 De Orellana sails down the Amazon.

1611 Hudson dies trying to find the Northwest Passage.

1682 De la Salle journeys down the Mississippi.

1768–1779 Captain Cook explores the south Pacific and discovers Australia.

1796 Park reaches the Niger River.

1804–1806 Lewis & Clark (below) cross North America.

1853–1856 David Livingstone crosses Africa.

1858 John Speke discovers Lake Victoria.

1860–1861 Burke & Wills cross Australia.

1867–1877 Przewalski explores Central Asia.

1911 Amundsen wins the race to the South Pole, beating Scott.

1930 Amy Johnson flies solo from England to Australia.

1953 Norgay and Hillary climb Mt Everest.

1960 Piccard sinks to the deepest point in the ocean.

1969 Armstrong walks on the Moon.

2020 The first manned mission to Mars (*right*)?

INDEX

Photocredits (*Abbreviations: t – top, m – middle, b – bottom, l – left, r – right*).
Cover, 4-5, 9t, 14 both, 19m, 20b, 21t, 22b, 23t, 27t, 28t, 29t, 33t, 34m, 36m: Mary Evans Picture Library. 6t, 15, 18, 26, 29b, 30, 34t, 35t, 37b, 38b, 43b, 45b: Frank Spooner Pictures. 6b, 12, 20 –21, 43, 45m: Ronald Grant Archive. 7 both, 11t, 20t, 32t: AKG London. 8t, 9b, 10, 17t, 19b, 23b, 33m, 35m, 40, 41b, 44m: Kobal Collection. 11b: Ancient Art & Architecture Collection. 13b, 25t: Eye Ubiquitous. 17m: Solution Pictures. 22t, 29m: Roger Vlitos. 27m, 36t: Hutchison Library. 31: Bruce Coleman Collection. 36b, 38t, 39, 41t, 42: Hulton Getty Collection. 44t & b: NASA.